Grandma Always Said . . .

The Little Book of Farm Country Wisdom

Pearl Hummerding

Voyageur Press

Edited by Amy Rost-Holtz
Jacket designed by Maria Friedrich
Interior designed by Kjerstin Moody
Printed in Hong Kong

01 02 03 04 05 5 4 3 2 1

Library of Congress Catalog Card Number:
2001039018
ISBN: 0-89658-568-9

Distributed in Canada by Raincoast Books
9050 Shaughnessy Street
Vancouver, B.C. V6P 6E5

Published by Voyageur Press, Inc.
123 North Second Street, P.O. Box 338
Stillwater, MN 55082 U.S.A.
651-430-2210, fax 651-430-2211
books@voyageurpress.com
www.voyageurpress.com

*Educators, fundraisers, premium and gift buyers,
publicists, and marketing managers:* Looking for
creative products and new sales ideas?
Voyageur Press books are available at special
discounts when purchased in quantities, and
special editions can be created to your
specifications. For details contact the
marketing department at 800-888-9653.

Endsheets: *Sisters put their hands to the task in 1928.*

Frontispiece: *Venus on a Farmall: An Indiana farm wife takes the wheel of
the family tractor during the soybean harvest.*

Title page: *Grandma's wash day became infinitely less laborious when gas-
powered stationary engines came along to power the wringer washer.*

Acknowledgments

Thank you to all the folks who—intentionally or unwittingly—contributed sayings to this collection: Margret Aldrich, John O. Allen, Ida May Blage, Thelma Bowen, Darlene Cornell, Kari Cornell, Michael Dregni, Maria Fredrich, Deb Gruebele, Haidi Hanson, Dave Hohman, Reuben Holtz, Laverne Hommerding, Mary LaBarre, Bonnie McCormack, Vincent Nell, Arthur Peterson, Lorraine Peterson, Christine Snow, and Rebecca Zins.

J. C. Allen & Son's extensive collection of rural photographs spans three generations, from approximately 1904 to the present. Photographs from this collection make up Voyageur Press's *Pictures from the Farm*. They have also appeared in Voyageur Press's *This Old Farm*, *A Farm Country Christmas*, *100 Years of Vintage Farm Tractors*, and *The Complete Pig*.

To the Reader

My grandma has seen a lot and learned a lot in her eighty-plus years, a perspective which has earned her the right (she says) to offer bits of advice to just about anyone in just about any circumstance. Sometimes her advice is solicited, sometimes it's not; sometimes it's welcome, sometimes it's not; sometimes it's applicable, sometimes it's not. It is always, however, free and abundant.

My grandma is both a daughter and a bride of central Wisconsin dairy farmers. She grew up during the lean years of the Great Depression, watched her own children grow up during the 1950s and 1960s, and for the past three decades has been watching them raise her grandchildren.

Although she and my grandfather sold the family farm and have lived "in town" for some thirty-odd years, her words of wisdom retain the color and flavor of the hard-working, no-nonsense farm lifestyle. As she often says—sometimes self-mockingly, but more often with pride—"You can take the girl off the farm, but you can't take the farm out of the girl."

Facing page: A young woman models the bib overalls and comfortable shoes that were de rigueur *on American farms of the 1950s.*

I've found this to be true of many current and former farmers. And in an age of experts and psychologists and self-help books and support groups, the down-home, farm-country words of wisdom of people like my grandma are refreshing in their forthrightness, honesty, and brevity.

I compiled this book to bring sundry pieces of that wisdom together. Like farm folks and their wisdom, it is forthright, honest, and to the point.

Not all the sayings are from my own grandma; many of them were uttered by other farm-country grandparents and passed along to me by in-laws, co-workers, friends, and friends of friends. Some of the sayings are familiar and well known, others are unique. Some are common sense, others seem to make little sense. Some are literal, others use aspects of the farm as a metaphor for a greater truth. Some are reflections of the values of yesteryear, others are timeless and sage advice for even the most modern and urbane lives.

This book is for my grandma, and for grandmas everywhere, who, whether by nature or nurture, willingly share their wisdom and never mince their words.

Pearl Hummerding

Facing page: *"Idle hands do the devil's work,"* *many a grandma always said. Fortunately, the rigors of farm life leave little time for hands to fall idle. (Courtesy of Dave Hohman)*

"Less talk, more work."

Father-son bonding, as it was done down on the farm.

"Many hands make light work."

In the 1890s and early 1900s, the harvest brought far-flung farm neighbors together in community threshing crews. (*Fred Hulstrand History in Pictures Collection, NDIRS-NDSU, Fargo*)

"Farmers raise their own help."

Large families were common on many North American farms. (Minnesota Historical Society)

"A child that doesn't work ain't worth the food you put in him."

With so much work to do, even the littlest hands became farm hands. Many farm kids credit their upbringing with teaching them the value of hard work.

"A man works from sun to sun, but a woman's work is never done."

Before the days of electricity and indoor plumbing, doing laundry was a major undertaking. (Fred Hulstrand History in Pictures Collection, NDIRS-NDSU, Fargo)

"On the farm, there's no such thing as men's work and women's work. There's just hard work and lots of it."

Two Indiana farm women pitch in by pitching oats into the threshing machine.

"Make hay while the sun shines."

Tractors and baling machines made bringing in hay easier, but it still isn't a job that can be done in the dark.

"There's no such thing as hibernation for farmers. Or tractors."

Equipped with snow chains and a plow, this Allis-Chalmers works year round.

"The worse it smells, the better it works."

A 1950s farmer uses his Farmall to load manure.

"If you don't use your head, you have to use your feet."

A valuable life lesson depicted in the art of a 1955 International Harvester calendar.

"Water tastes best after a hard day's work."

A swig from the water jug offered brief relief from a day of hot, dusty air in the wheat fields.

"Take your time, but hurry up."

The rough state of early country highways forced many speed demons to slow down and take their time.

"The squeaky wheel gets the grease."

An Indiana farmer gets ready to head out to the fields by greasing the wheels of the plow.

"There's a time for work and a time for play."

A father and son take time off to enjoy a warm summer day at the farmstead fishing hole. This evocative artwork graced the cover of a 1950s Massey-Harris Buyers' Guide.

"Everyone needs a hobby."

A North Dakota farm woman displays her collection of Norwegian spinning wheels in 1940. (Fred Hulstrand History in Pictures Collection, NDIRS-NDSU, Fargo)

"Busy hands are happy hands."

Harmony in the home, in more ways than one. (Fred Hulstrand History in Pictures Collection, NDIRS-NDSU, Fargo)

"Any job worth doing is worth doing well."

A quilter displays her prize-winning work at the 1926 Minnesota State Fair. (Minnesota State Fair collection)

"Give credit where credit is due."

Mom and her blue-ribbon-winning peaches get the royal treatment on the way home from the county fair in this 1952 calendar artwork.

"It ain't braggin' if you can do it."

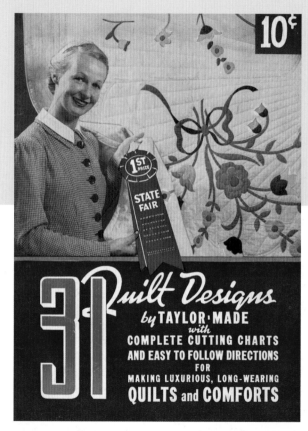

You too can brag, if you follow Taylor-Made's vintage quilt directions and charts.

10¢

1ST PRIZE
STATE FAIR

31 *Quilt Designs*
by **TAYLOR·MADE**
with
COMPLETE CUTTING CHARTS
AND EASY TO FOLLOW DIRECTIONS
FOR
MAKING LUXURIOUS, LONG-WEARING
QUILTS and **COMFORTS**

"Sit up straight and keep your legs crossed."

Best wishes for a prosperous 1939. Minnie Moline

Miss Minnie Moline practices proper posture and deportment in this 1939 promotional pinup for tractor manufacturer Minneapolis-Moline. (Minnesota Historical Society)

"A good pie crust is the sign of a good woman."

Wearing her trusty 4-H apron, a farm matron rolls out another perfect crust for her homemade pies.

"The way to a man's heart is through his stomach."

A covered picnic basket and a winsome wave lures Pa in from the field in this vintage painting by Walter Haskell Hinton.

"Women love men who dance."

Couples cut a rug at a 1950s country dance.

"Men love women who drive tractor."

A young suitor introduces his beau to the tractor seat at a 1950s Minnesota State Fair. (Minnesota State Fair collection)

"If you want to know how a man will treat you, look at the way he treats his tractor."

A 1930s farmer carefully covers his tractor with a tarp while it is in storage.

"Marry the one who makes you smile."

Sweethearts enjoy a leisurely stroll along a country stream on their way to a romantic picnic spot.

"Behind every great farmer is a great farm wife."

The bigger the boy, the bigger the rips. Why take your britches off if you're just going to have to put them back on again? (Glenbow Archives, Calgary, Canada, PA-1875-2689)

> "Spending a little time together each day will keep the romance alive."

After a hard day of farm work, Ma and Pa relax together with rocking chairs and a radio program.

"Always greet your husband with a warm smile and a hot meal."

From the distinctive note of the Johnny Popper's engine, farm wives could tell when their husbands had idled down the tractor to come in for supper. Deere & Company featured this painting by Walter Haskell Hinton in one of its promotional calendars. (Deere & Company archives)

> "Always wear a clean apron at mealtime—a dirty cook spoils the appetite."

The colorful artwork of a 1952 farm implement calendar captures the sense of anticipation surrounding Sunday dinner.

> "A watched pot never boils. But an unwatched pot boils over."

Watching the pot was only half the job for a cook using a wood stove such as this one. She also had to keep the fire well stoked with firewood or corncobs.

"Keep a level head and a level cup."

The experienced chef knows precise measurements are essential to making tasty homemade ice cream.

"You can never baste a turkey too many times."

The family's Thanksgiving turkey needs one more drizzle of drippings and a few more minutes in the cast-iron oven before it is ready for the table.

"Your hands can't be too clean when you're baking bread."

Using her apron as oven mitts, a grandma takes fresh-baked loaves from an old-time wood-fired oven.

"Always use the freshest ingredients."

Wielding a hatchet with a steady hand was a practical and necessary skill on the farm, where the first step in preparing a fried-chicken dinner usually was stretching the bird's neck out on the chopping block.

"Use everything but the squeal."

No part of a butchered hog was wasted. The head could be boiled for head cheese or its meat chopped up for mincemeat; the fat was cut into cubes and rendered into lard; the hams and loins were cured with salt and smoke; other meat trimmings were made into sausage. Parts that wouldn't keep were eaten immediately.

"Eat what you can, can what you can't."

Just about any fruit or vegetable, as well as meat, is fit to be canned. Canning was an essential part of farm life, especially in areas where winter prevented the fields and gardens from producing all year round.

> "Always have a well-stocked pantry, just in case things get bad."

Most farm families of the early to mid twentieth century kept their pantries well stocked to provide extra food for when company visited or in case of lean times. (Glenbow Archives, Calgary, Canada, NA-1367-62)

"Cook to suit yourself—the family will eat it."

Bringing lunch to Dad in the field was often easier and more efficient than having him drive the Farmall and combine all the way back to the farmyard. But even the most makeshift picnic included coffee and cake.

"If you put it on your plate, you eat it."

Farm kids' eyes were not allowed to be bigger than their stomachs.

"Sunday dinners are like church—they're both good for the soul."

And, as with church, you were expected to dress up, be quiet, and behave at the Sunday dinner table.

"Food tastes better with friends."

Church potlucks or covered-dish dinners provided a chance for far-flung rural neighbors to socialize.

"Mom's medicine is the best medicine."

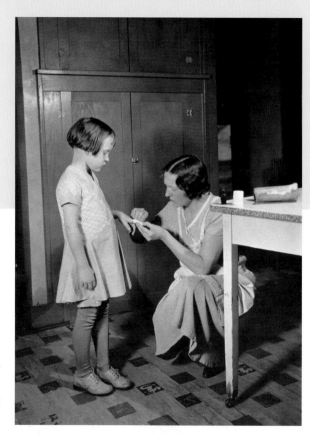

A clean dressing, plus a kiss and a hug from Mom, takes the sting out of most scrapes and cuts.

"A good beating builds character."

In the days before wall-to-wall carpeting, rugs had to be cleaned by hauling them outside and beating the dirt loose.

> "Rags may not turn into riches, but they make good rugs."

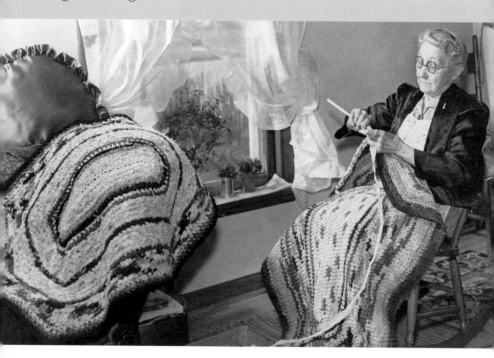

In the farm tradition of "waste not, want not," clothes were worn until they were completely worn out, then recycled into rags and rugs.

"A stitch in time saves nine."

Nimble fingers were necessary to keep the clothes of an active farm family in good repair.

"It's no disgrace to have patches on your clothes, so long as they're clean."

Clothes were near impossible to keep clean down on the farm: As soon as they were donned after a serious washing, they were worn into the fields to get dirty all over again.

> "Wind is free and clothes pins are cheap."

Even after electricity and clothes dryers arrived in the farmhouse, many frugal farm wives still made the most of sunny summer days to hang out the wash.

"Don't be afraid to try new things."

SEE WHAT'S NEW FOR _YOU_ IN PYREX WARE!

PYREX WARE sets the style for wartime cooking! Every useful glass PYREX utensil serves you in a dozen different ways. Take it from stove to dinner table to refrigerator with no stops for dishwashing in between! You save time because foods bake as much as one-third faster...saving fuel! Let PYREX WARE help make your daily meals exciting...add new charm to home entertaining!

NEW

FOR THE FIRST TIME... A PIE PLATE WITH EASY-TO-HOLD HANDLES!

CONVENIENT GLASS HANDLES HELP YOU IN BAKING AND SERVING

FLUTED EDGE MAKES YOUR CRUSTS ATTRACTIVE

"Pyrex Ware sets the style for wartime cooking!" declares this ad from the 1940s, as it introduced cooks to a revolutionary new baking tool: "A pie plate with easy-to-hold handles!"

"You're never too old to try something new."

NEW DAY ON THE FARM

FARMALL is a registered trade-mark.
ONLY International Harvester builds FARMALL Tractors.

FARMALL *CUB* IS HERE
with Matched Cub Equipment!

"Faster, easier work—all-purpose capacity and economy" is what a 1947 International Harvester ad promised its Farmall Cub would bring to the small farms of America.

> "'I don't know how to do that' is no excuse. You can do anything if you put your mind to it."

An ambitious young farmer takes on a formidable Minneapolis-Moline GB Diesel. Learning to pilot a tractor solo was a rite of passage for many farm kids. (Minnesota State Fair collection)

> "Go outside every day, even if it's cold. The fresh air will do you good."

A skating party is one way to get your daily dose of fresh air during the winter. Many farmers of the early twentieth century also believed in bringing the fresh air indoors by throwing open the windows—even in the coldest months—to air out the house.

"Share and share alike."

This Massey-Harris 44 is big enough for all its curious admirers to try out at once. (Voyageur Press archives)

> "Listen to your elders."

A grandfather shows his grandson how to hoe a straight row and plant potato slips by hand.

"You gotta know what's a good deal and what's not."

You're never to young to learn about good values.

"Make do with what you have."

With a blow torch, elbow grease, and little bit of ingenuity, a Ford Model T automobile could be transformed into a homemade tractor or "doodlebug."

"Sometimes you have to make your own fun."

A resourceful farm family takes a whirl on their homemade merry-go-round, the "Flying Jinney."

"You don't need fancy-schmancy toys on the farm."

A massive haystack, a dog, and a couple of playmates were often all a farm kid needed to have fun.

"Fun is where you find it."

It may not be a Cinderella-style carriage, but riding an ox-drawn binder can make a girl feel like a princess of the wheat fields, as the North Dakota woman in this early-1900s photograph can attest. (Fred Hustrand History in Pictures Collection, NDIRS-NDSU, Fargo)

"It's the little things that make life worthwhile."

A young girl gets an affectionate nibble from her white piglet. Taking care of small animals was one way younger family members could help out around the farm.

"We all need a little help sometimes."

A mother farm dog gets a break while her pups get a little extra milk.

"Sometimes you go solo. Sometimes you're part of the band."

Growing up as part of a large farm family taught kids the value of cooperation in both work and play.

> "You can lead a horse to water—and if he's thirsty enough, he'll drink."

Before the advent of steam- and gas-powered tractors, horses were farmers' partners, spending long days with them in the fields. Horses were often treated as family pets as well.

"Cows don't care what you wear. They just care if your hands are warm."

Old coveralls, overalls, and boots are usually the best things to wear to the dairy barn, but sometimes there just isn't time to change before the milking needs to be done.

"Don't put all your eggs in one basket."

No conveyer belts or cages here. Before the days of large, commercial chicken-farming operations, farmers rustled through nests twice a day to pick out each egg and collect them in baskets.

> "Don't count your chickens before they're hatched.
But after they're hatched, count 'em twice."

*Flats of baby chicks
arriving at the brooder
house was a sign of spring
on the farm.*

"No sense buying the chicken if you can get the eggs for free."

Taking care of livestock and poultry gave farm kids a firsthand education on the cycles of birth, life, death, and all natural happenings in between.

"If we had some eggs, we'd have ham and eggs—if we had some ham."

Eggs were a staple at the farm table, and an average farm family could go through a dozen a week, if not more. So farms usually kept a healthy-sized flock of hens, and with a big enough flock, there might be some eggs left over to sell to the local farm co-op or grocery store.

"If you spend too much time wondering which came first, you'll never get your chores done."

Known for laying a high number of eggs per hen, White Leghorns are one of the most popular poultry breeds on North American poultry farms.

"If you eat as many as you pick, you'll have to pick twice as many."

A farm boy pauses to enjoy the fruits of his labor.

"You know it's autumn when you see corn shocks and pumpkins."

In the early days of North American farming, the first step in the corn harvest was to cut the stalks and bind them into bundles, then the bundles were stood on end and stacked together in shocks until they dried.

"Good things come in threes."

The family pony gives three youngsters their first lesson in horsemanship.

"A true friend is more precious than gold."

All saddled up, Billy the Kid gets set for a ride on Billy the kid.

"A raggedy ride beats a dressed-up walk."

Laugh all you want. What this two-wheeled carriage lacks in elegance it makes up for in practicality.

> "Birds of a feather flock together."

And sometimes they flock in the most unusual places. Fortunately, most farm kids are well accustomed to the ways of animals.

> "Beauty is in the eye of the beholder."

John C. Allen, the first of three generations of J. C. Allen & Son photographers, found beauty in the seemingly ordinary aspects of rural life and preserved it in his photographs.

"You gotta eat a peck of dirt before you die."

Many farmsteads began with a sod house, such as this one, built in North Dakota in the 1920s. (Fred Hulstrand History in Pictures Collection, NDIRS-NDSU, Fargo)

"There's dirt and there's soil. Dirt is what you sweep up off the kitchen floor. Soil is the life of the farm."

A father and son collect soil samples just before planting time. Testing the soil's acidity and nutrient levels help determine which type of fertilizer should be applied for maximum production.

"There's no place like home."

The joy and relief of returning to a warm, glowing farmhouse after chores is depicted in this artwork from a 1951 International Harvester promotional calendar.

"The family that farms together, stays together."

A proud farm family portrait: Mom, Dad, son, and a Minneapolis-Moline U Series tractor. (Minnesota Historical Society)

"Anyone can farm, but not everyone is a farmer."

This artwork, from a 1952 International Harvester promotional calendar, captures the excitement as the whole family, from the kids to the dog to the geese, come to investigate Dad's latest purchase: a Farmall H.